PEASANT DESIGNS

FOR ARTISTS AND CRAFTSMEN

PEASANT DESIGNS

FOR ARTISTS AND CRAFTSMEN

by Ed Sibbett, Jr.

Dover Publications, Inc., New York

Published in Canada by General Publishing Company, Ltd., 30 Lesmill Road, Don Mills, Toronto, Ontario.
Published in the United Kingdom by Constable and Company, Ltd., 10 Orange Street, London WC2H 7EG.

Peasant Designs for Artists and Craftsmen is a new work, first published by Dover Publications, Inc., in 1977.

DOVER *Pictorial Archive* SERIES

International Standard Book Number: 0-486-23478-9
Library of Congress Catalog Card Number: 76-58079

Manufactured in the United States of America
Dover Publications, Inc.
180 Varick Street
New York, N.Y. 10014

Publisher's Note

The vigorous peasant designs of Central and Eastern Europe have long been an inspiration to artists, designers, decorators and craftsmen. The 255 examples in the present volume have been redrawn or recreated in a deft and clean pen technique for immediate usability. The original designs appeared on textiles, ceramics, furniture and many other art and craft objects. There are florals, animals, birds and human figures in elaborate folk costumes, as well as picturesque borders, frames and corners.

The drawings are based on pictorial material in the following publications:

Bossert, Helmuth T., *Ornamente der Volkskunst: Gewebe, Teppiche, Stickereien* [Ornament in Folk Art: Textiles, Carpets, Embroidery], Verlag Ernst Wasmuth, Tübingen, 1949.

Broderies et décoration populaires tchéco-slovaques [Czechoslovak Folk Embroidery and Ornament], portfolio published by H. Ernst, Paris, n.d. [ca. 1920].

Fél, Edit; Tamás Hofer & Klára K.-Csilléry, *Hungarian Peasant Art*, Corvina Press, Budapest, 1958.

Gink, Károly, & Ivor Sándor Kiss, *Folk Art and Folk Artists in Hungary*, Corvina Press, Budapest, 1968.

Malonyay, Dezső, *A magyar nép művészete* [Hungarian Folk Art], Franklin-Társulat, Budapest, vols. 2, 3 & 4, 1909, 1911 & 1912.

Mann, Kathleen, *Design from Peasant Art*, Adam & Charles Black, London, 1939.

Sič, Albert, *Narodni okraski na orodju in pohištvu* [Folk Decoration on Utensils and Furniture], J. Blasnik's Successors, Ljubljana [Yugoslavia], 1923 [Slovenian folk art].

Sič, Albert, *Narodni okraski na pirhih in kožuhih* [Folk Decoration on Easter Eggs and Sheepskin Coats], J. Blasnik's Successors, Ljubljana, 1922 [Slovenian].

PEASANT DESIGNS

FOR ARTISTS AND CRAFTSMEN

4

48

48

56

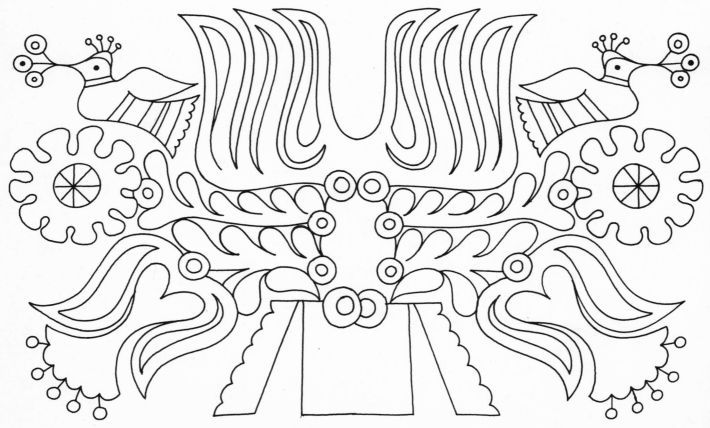

92